A HOUSE
OF ORDER

Daryl V. Hoole

A HOUSE OF ORDER

Deseret Book
Salt Lake City, Utah

ISBN 0-87747-597-0
Library of Congress Catalog Card Number 84-72520

First printing November 1984

Contents

Preface

For more than twenty-five years I have done a great deal of speaking and writing about personal and home management. Traditionally my efforts have been focused primarily toward the mother. Circumstances have changed in many homes, however, requiring fathers to be more active and involved in the management of the home and the rearing of children. There are more single men and women and single parents responsible for homes than ever before. Therefore, this book, which is an update and a consolidation of my earlier books, *The Art of Homemaking* and *The Joys of Homemaking*, is dedicated to everyone who seeks the rewards of effective personal and home management.

Introduction

Homemakers everywhere—men and women—repeatedly ask the same questions: "What is it that works so well for you and your family?" "Can you tell us in a short, specific way what helps at your house?" "What makes the difference?"

The answer to all of these questions can be found in the counsel of the Lord: "Organize yourselves; prepare every needful thing; and establish a house, even a house of prayer, a house of fasting, a house of faith, a house of learning, a house of glory, a house of order, a house of God." (D&C 88:119.) I'd like to recommend six keys to creating "a house of order":

1. Be orderly and organized.
2. Be efficient.
3. Do first things first.
4. Get the notebook habit.
5. Enlist the family's cooperation.
6. Be of good cheer.

You might add to this list several keys of your own that you know you can rely on and repeat and make an integral part of your life and home management. The important thing is to find out what works for *you*. Some people have good days or bad days and don't really know why. They don't know the rules of home management and therefore they hit and miss in their efforts. This reminds me of a woman who says her homemade bread turns out only 20 percent of the time. She knows a lot about what causes failure but not much about what works.

Before discussing the keys to "what works," however, let's define a couple of terms and mention a few of the rules for failure and some of the joys of success.

Success in the home indicates that it is a clean, orderly, attractive, comfortable abode that is designed and managed to bring out the very best in people and help them achieve their full potential in health and happiness, growth and progress. It is a place where people like to be.

On the other hand, failure in the home is often represented by clutter, neglect, uncleanliness, and situations and conditions that foster weakness, rather than strength, in people.

Some people struggle with homemaking responsibilities and fail to varying degrees because they literally don't know how to keep house. They grew up without proper role models or effective training, or somehow just failed to develop the skills and habits to do the job. The matter can be solved, however, if they are determined enough to seek answers from books and classes and experienced homemakers, and then are disciplined enough to apply what they've learned. Many people do have that kind of determination and discipline and are able to turn failure into success in their homes.

Some homemakers who fall short in their homemaking are lazy and unmotivated. They do practically nothing when they should be doing something, or they use illness or various projects and activities as an excuse for neglect or as an escape from responsibility. Such women need a lot of help, encouragement, and appreciation. The matter can be solved by a change in attitude and priorities, by using incentive programs, by working on improvement of skills.

Sometimes difficult circumstances, such as long-term illness, inconvenient housing and living conditions, extremely demanding schedules, or other complications, cause a breakdown in homemaking and family life. These problems are solved by complete cooperation and extra help from the entire family. There are beautiful examples of parents and children uniting and doing the almost impossible together. Whatever the problem, it can be well compensated for by the love and harmony the family members experience through their united efforts.

Some homemakers keep lovely homes, but that's all they do—it takes all their time. They are slaves to their houses. These homemakers need help in sharpening up their skills, and they need some activities and projects to serve as incentives to help them move a little faster.

Now, on the positive side, countless homemakers find great success and satisfaction through their homemaking. They function quickly and well. They know the rules and make them work. They have the attitudes, habits, and skills required to do the job well. They make their homes look good, and in turn their homes make them look good—something we all can use for our self-respect. And interestingly enough, it's usually the homemakers with the cleanest, neatest homes who have the most time to do the extras—to enhance the quality of life for everyone concerned. They know the rewards of having homes of order. Just as there is infinite value in taking care of one's mind and body, so there is a great deal of peace and progress to be had in caring for one's possessions. It is important for us to care well for what we have.

Good homemakers have learned that it's really easier to keep house than it is not to. They don't make messes for themselves. They are ahead, rather than behind, in their work and consequently in their lives. Things are less likely to be lost, spilled, or broken. Time, money, and strength are at their optimum.

In short, homes that look good enhance self-respect; homes that function well are conducive to maximum progress for all family members; and positive attitudes, habits, skills, and values are perpetuated for another generation.

But there is a more important motivation—perhaps the most significant reason of all—for being a good homemaker. I am greatly sustained by the belief that I'm not just keeping house; rather, I'm making a home to last forever. The concept of eternal family life makes all the difference for me. I'm not sure it would be worth it just to keep house. I'm afraid all the diapers, dishes, and dust I've handled over the years with eight children would have gotten me down were it not for the fact that I have known I am building beyond that. I'm working for an eternal family to love and an eternal home to keep. For that I'd pay any price.

As you can see, I keep house for several reasons. To help others in their desire to do so, I enthusiastically recommend these six keys. It has worked beautifully for us. Ours has been a busy household, yet through the years we've had a happy, orderly home (most of the time) where everyone and everything has received our best. Knowing what works and then relying on it, repeating it every day, has made this so.

It has been said that a person's character can be determined by what that individual does when he or she doesn't have to do anything. The keys in this book are to give us the time and energy to improve the quality of our lives and those of our families, rather than to make us bored, restless, or discontent, or to waste our time with empty pleasures. These are the keys to having time for becoming a more informed, interested, cultured, spiritual person; for becoming a more loving and companionable marriage partner; for being a more effective parent; for becoming a more sensitive, thoughtful, helpful neighbor and friend; for being of greater service in our church and community; for being a more consistent scripture reader, a more faithful journal and family record keeper, and a more regular temple attender. It's when we feel good about ourselves and the house—when the dishes are done, the laundry is caught up, the house is in order, and the children are under control—that individuals and families do their best growing.

Please consider these six keys, add to or subtract from them to meet your needs most effectively, and then, with this as *your* success formula, make it work. The effort is truly worthwhile, because, as Winston Churchill said, "We shape our houses and then our houses shape us."

Key 1

Be Orderly and Organized

An eminent scientist once said that it takes intelligence to create order. If that's the case, what it takes to make a mess is quite obvious! We ought to compliment ourselves by keeping order all about us.

Order is power, order is peace, order is progress. Many good things are based on order. An orderly, attractive, well-cared-for home does a lot for one's self-respect, and never before have we needed to guard our self-respect as carefully as we do right now. There are forces at large in the world attempting to undermine feelings of self-worth, and the tool the adversary uses to mislead the righteous is discouragement. A cluttered house can be extremely discouraging.

Order also affects the atmosphere in the home. For example, family members are usually a lot more pleasant when the cellophane tape or the car keys can be quickly located. Whatever the project, purpose, or activity, things are soon done in an orderly home, whether it's a one-room apartment or a fourteen-room mansion. And when we take good care of what we have, we can use our money to improve our life-styles rather than to replace broken, lost, or abused items.

When a home reflects tender loving care, everyone benefits. Better homes make better people. The quality of the home is not determined by how expensive or large it is, but by what kind of living takes place there. Disarray brings out the worst in people; orderliness encourages our best.

I learned an important lesson about order a few years ago, when I was having babies. I always attended demonstrations at the hospital to learn more about the care of infants. One particular time the demonstration was conducted by an experienced, seasoned nursery nurse. She had been working some thirty years and knew almost all there was to know about babies. She gave us young mothers some very helpful counsel and advice that day: "Mothers, teach your babies an orderly way of life. It will be greatly to their advantage. The time to do it is right now. As you take your babies home from the hospital, select a time—it doesn't matter when it is, morning, noon, or evening—for your baby's bath and then consistently bathe your baby at that same time every day. The reason for this is that a baby's bath is the most dramatic event of his day, and he will regulate his life around that bath time. If the bath time is hit and miss and on and off, the poor baby will be confused. If the bath time is consistent, nearly every baby will adjust to a schedule. The baby will really sleep, rather than just catnap, and will really eat, rather than just snack. He will be happy and contented. Otherwise the baby will be irritable and you'll likely be exhausted and miss much of the joy that otherwise would come." Of course, other factors can influence the matter, and some babies won't settle down no matter what parents do, but the great majority of them respond to this.

If order is that important in a tiny baby's life, how vital it must be for the whole family! We could go on and on discussing the value of order, but let's leave the theories and discuss *how* to achieve it. It's important to organize things first; then time management follows quite naturally. Here, then, are a few ideas for putting things in order.

1. Have a place for everything and keep everything in its place.

This phrase is terribly trite, but it's still true and it still works. We all can say it; some people do it. I must hasten to point out that toys don't count! A baby's playthings scattered about the house are not offensive. That's just part of having a toddler. That is acceptable—unless the baby is fifteen years old! What is offensive is to see the clutter of grown-ups who should know better. Such items need to be put away or thrown away, whatever is required.

Smart home managers practice the picking-up process as they go about their homes and yards. Taking a second here and there to pick up and throw away or put away an out-of-place item adds up to an orderly home. Good housekeeping is not as much a matter of cleaning house as it is of *keeping* house.

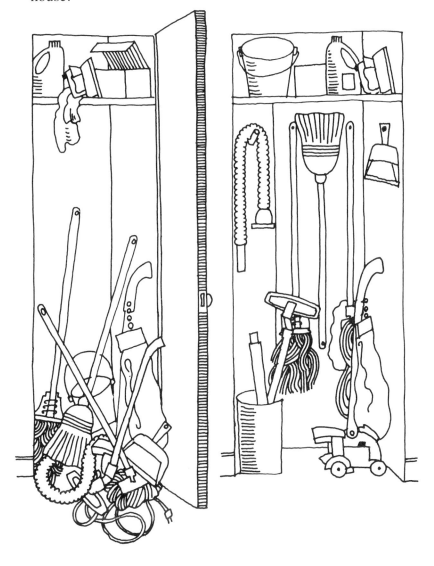

Clutter attracts clutter. If no one puts the first item (which shouldn't be there) on the dining room table, or on the mantel, or on the top of the refrigerator, family members are less likely to put the second and third and finally the tenth item there.

If our house lacks sufficient cupboards and closets, we can increase our storage space by investing in or improvising step-shelves, half-shelves, drawer dividers, racks, hooks, and so forth. Attractive, durable household organizers are available in all sorts of shapes, sizes, and colors for more compact living.

In storing items away, these three rules are helpful: (1) Place items in containers so we see them only when we need them. For instance, if we want to save bows and ribbons from gift packages to reuse, we can keep them together out of the way in some type of large container. (2) Set limits on what we store. It's not productive to keep more than we actually use. For example, I save plastic and foil cartons to take food to neighbors and friends who are ill or lonely or for some reason need a little attention. They appreciate the disposable containers (it can be such an inconvenience to have to return dishes), and I'm relieved by not having to keep track of dishes all over the neighborhood. But I keep on hand only a dozen or so of these containers, not hundreds of them. (3) It's really smart to keep a master list of what we store so we know, without even looking, what is in the attic or at the back of a closet.

Toys can be more fun and less frustrating for both parents and children if they're contained in small drawstring bags or plastic cartons rather than in toy boxes where they turn to instant junk. The cords from the bags can be tied in knots to prevent the children or their playmates from dumping the toys and disrupting the whole system. Individual containers can look colorful and attractive in a play area, conserve space, and keep toys well organized so children can play with them for the purpose for which they are intended. For example, few children have the patience to sort through a box of

toys to get together enough little plastic bricks to build something. If the pieces are not sorted and manageable, the children will just dump the box and make a mess.

The system of using individual containers also helps children pace their play—otherwise they might go through all their toys the first ten minutes of the day. Further, the toys can be rotated so that the children don't see every toy every day. When a bag is opened after not having been used for several weeks, the toys it contains are almost like new to the children. Best of all, the bags and containers come with a rule: No new bags or containers can be opened until the contents of the last one (or several containers, depending on the toys needed for play) have been picked up. This makes picking up part of the game, instead of a tiresome task at the end of the day when the children are tired and the parent is harried and when it takes time from a bedtime story and visit.

We can make it a point to give our children (or grandchildren) appropriate containers as they receive new toys, and be firm in teaching them to pick up what has been played with before going on to the next project. This bit of care and organization can keep toys and games in good order for years, keep our house more free of clutter, and provide maximum enjoyment for our children.

2. Organize keepsakes as well as possessions.

Great personal satisfaction and choice family experiences can come from keeping family records, journals, and albums in order and current. Movie films, slide shows, video tapes, and cassette tapes should be cataloged and labeled. Doing this can be a highly rewarding project for the entire family; Sundays, holidays, and winter evenings are ideal times.

Along this same line, it's a wonderful idea to prepare a keepsake box or treasure chest for each of our children. All we need is some sort of container (empty orange or apple boxes with secure tops, obtained from the grocery store, make inexpensive ones) covered with the child's favorite color or design in fabric or stick-on paper. Such a keepsake box does much more than provide a child with a specific place for valuables: it also gives him a deep sense of security. In order to have hopes and dreams for the future, everyone needs some memories of the past.

It's invaluable to have home filing systems for recipes, important papers, or any collection of materials. Remember, a system is a lot better than the search. And it's going to be one or the other in every home; the choice is ours. (Detailed instructions for filing things and then finding them again can be found in the appendix.)

3. Put it away if it is not part of the decor.

Unless something is attractive, we can eliminate clutter by keeping it out of sight as far as is practical. My home is my world, the place where I spend most of my time. Even though the big world out there is confusing and full of problems, my world can be just as peaceful, pleasant, and lovely as our family makes it. We are in charge there. I believe that clutter is paralyzing and demoralizing. Pretty paint doesn't cost any more than ugly paint does. Furthermore, I believe that anyone's house can be attractive, because good taste knows no price tag. Beautiful homes are not made of money, but are the result of just picking up, putting away, polishing off, and painting up.

Even the most humble home can be transformed into magazine material with some ideas and ambition. Arrangements of grasses or leaves in battered tin cans can be decorative; healthy plants do wonders for bare spots; homemade quilts and pillows can quickly brighten up a room; refinished furniture from someone's attic or garage can become priceless. It just takes a little vision and work. A nicely decorated home does infinitely more for our feelings of self-respect and well-being than does one that is "decorated" with aerosol cans on windowsills or cracker boxes on the kitchen counter or "centerpieces" of somebody's backpack or laundry on mantels and tables.

4. Avoid putting twenty-five pounds of stuff in a five-pound house.

In other words, keep the house "de-junked." If there's any cure-all for problem housekeeping, this is undoubtedly it. In fact, I've seen serious family problems solved by some

well-filled and well-disposed-of plastic garbage bags. Only at that point can the house begin to function and serve the needs of the people who live there.

Throwing things out or giving them away can take a great deal of courage, but the more we do it, the easier it will become. Each Tuesday morning as we set out the trash cans at our curb, our good neighbor across the street reminds us that we really get our tax dollar's worth on garbage day. I feel good and warm all through as I fill containers to pass on to one of our local salvage organizations. I know I'll never have to pick those items up again, and they're going to help someone else.

5. Leave your house orderly whenever you retire for bed or leave the house.

It's such a boost to wake up to or come home to a neat, clean, orderly house. Our day is a success before we've even opened our eyes or put our feet on the floor. It means a lot to start out ahead rather than behind.

A creative mother in our neighborhood helps her young children understand this concept by saying to them, "Before you go to bed, we need to put the house to bed."

It's not what we do that makes us tired; it's what we have not done that is so exhausting. A day's work completed is really quite exhilarating. We just need to change our shoes and we're good for hours more. On the other hand, it's when we're about halfway through our work and we see we're not going to make it that our backs start to ache, our legs get tired, and our feet hurt. It's the pileup that gets us down. Baking cookies can be a rewarding experience unless we get cookies on top of lunch dishes and lunch on top of breakfast dishes—and then it's not fun anymore.

Women who work outside the home often say that when they return home at the close of their day on the job they are really tired, and it's terribly difficult to face another work load at home. It's like working a double shift every day. If they're met at home by clutter and crumbs and dishes and laundry piled up, they literally fall apart. Conversely, if they come home to a house that's in order, with even a dinner in the refrigerator all ready to be slipped in the oven, they get a second wind, so to speak, and suddenly they have strength and stamina to work some more.

We are more often emotionally tired than physically tired. We think we're physically tired because that's how we feel, but really it's our minds telling our bodies to give up, not the other way around. The way to overcome emotional fatigue is to have a success experience. And good home management provides those kinds of experiences. The better we do, the better we can keep on doing. Nothing succeeds like success.

6. Establish some house rules.

Every institution needs rules, and because homes are the most important of all, some rules must be in effect there. Rules help us feel protected; they tell us someone cares. Rules help make the world a safe place. Rules can make home a much happier, more loving, more productive place. It's smarter to run on prevention than cures.

We don't want to have so many rules that children feel they're living in a "no-no" institution or in a pressure cooker, but a few firmly enforced rules can benefit everyone. Following are several rules for good housekeeping that help in our homes:

1. Don't put it down; put it away.

2. Leave any area better than you found it. Considerate people don't litter.

3. Don't eat on foot—no meals on wheels. Why should three rooms have to be cleaned just because someone had a cracker? Snack mats (especially designated bath mats, towels, or little rugs) or cookie chairs (especially designated little chairs or stools) help toddlers and little children keep this rule in a happy way. Remember, children go through either your nerves or your ideas!

4. Wash and dress yourself and put your room in order

before family prayer and breakfast. This process seems to require minutes before breakfast and hours afterwards.

5. Make your bed, put your room and the bathroom in order, help with breakfast cleanup, and feed pets (this takes about five to ten minutes for most children) before you go to school, start to play, or become involved in any activity. (In some homes, musical practice is also required before school and other activities.)

6. Clean up after snacks.

7. Don't leave the bathroom until it's tidy.

8. Work on projects in an area where spills and spatters can easily be wiped up, and put supplies away when the project is completed.

Don't forget that it's a sign of intelligence to create order. Be that smart!

Key 2

Be Efficient

Numerous books have been written and countless rules have been made on the subject of efficiency. Summed up, they state: "Avoid making two jobs out of one."

A common problem among homemakers is that they make work for themselves by being careless, sloppy, negligent, or blind to the problem. They spill it and splash it, then have to clean it; they mess it up, then have to straighten it; they lose it, then have to find it.

For example, instead of wiping up spilled egg immediately from the kitchen counter, they allow it to spread to the vanilla bottle, then onto the cupboard shelf, and then to the door pull and the refrigerator handle, and finally to the light switch. The result is either a sticky kitchen or unnecessary cleaning.

They neglect to keep their outside porches and steps clean, and as a result, leaves, sand, dirt, Christmas tree needles, and other things are tracked in. I learned as a young bride that if I kept the porch swept, I didn't have to clean the house as often. Besides, a well-swept porch announces to passersby and callers that people who care live there.

Here are a few more specific principles that help a homemaker work more efficiently.

1. Handle things only once.

Inefficient people merely rearrange things (papers on a desk, articles in a closet) instead of dealing with them. Some people think they're cleaning the garage when in fact all they're doing is rearranging it! Almost invariably when I hear tribute paid to an outstanding leader, someone who has truly achieved and contributed, it's said of that person that he or she handles papers only once. While answering the mail, he or she makes notes, underlines sentences, dictates a memo, dials the phone, or rings for the secretary. That person does something, while less efficient people merely move papers from one side of their desk to the other.

This same principle applies to our work in the kitchen. Some people spend much of their time repeatedly picking dishes up and setting them down again. We have a little rule at our house that before we cook or eat (and we do a lot of both), the dishwasher is to be unloaded so it can be reloaded with the next activity. Why set the dishes down only to pick them up later and put them in the dishwasher? Why not just place them directly there? I've learned that the kitchen sink has a lot to do with my disposition. When it's clear, I feel great. When it's full of dishes, I feel frustrated. If I add to that a cluttered countertop, I can barely function. This frustration spills over to other family members until my negative emotions are felt throughout the entire family. Then everyone overreacts. Thus, I've learned that for the good of all, everyone must help manage well in the kitchen. By the way, this has nothing to do with how many people we feed or how much we cook. It's strictly a matter of how it's done. For me, it's imperative to keep ahead in the kitchen.

I use my dishwasher to the fullest to avoid a pileup in the kitchen. I appreciate a dishwasher because it saves me a thousand or more hours a year, because it destroys germs and we're all a lot healthier, and because it's a perfect hiding place for what otherwise would be cluttering the sink or counter. It multiplies my efficiency as a result. But if you don't have a dishwasher, you can still work smart in the kitchen by keeping hot, soapy water in the sink where dishes are carefully stacked and soaking for easier washing later.

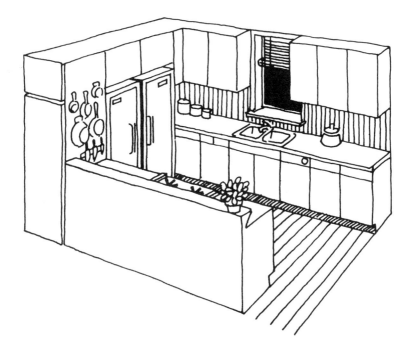

2. Arrange work and storage areas for maximum efficiency.

The overall arrangement of a kitchen is a major contributor toward efficiency. Plan your work so that it moves in one direction rather than back and forth, which wastes time and energy. If there's a choice, the ideal kitchen is a U-shaped one, with the range, refrigerator, and sink forming a triangle. Such an arrangement reduces steps and adds to counter and cupboard space.

If space is available, small, individual closets about a foot wide in an entryway provide excellent space for children's coats, caps, gloves, boots, lunch pails, school supplies, and sports equipment.

Efficiency in the laundry can also be achieved if the utility area is arranged effectively. Sorting bins or containers in which family members deposit their own soiled clothing can save the homemaker steps. Place containers for freshly laundered clothing (plastic dishpans, for instance) for individual family members above the washer, dryer, and folding area. When the containers are full, family members themselves take them to their rooms, place the contents in their closets and drawers, and return the containers to the utility area. This keeps the utility area free from stacks of clothing and saves the homemaker many steps in running from room to room with clean clothing.

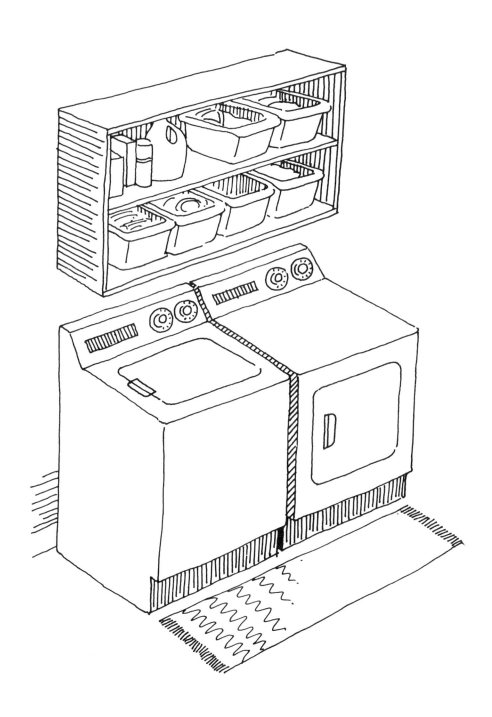

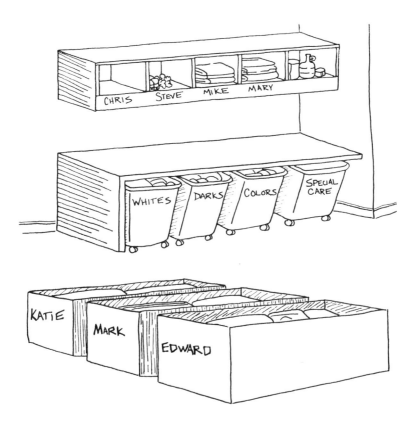

3. Avoid flitting.

At best, there are countless interruptions in a home-maker's day. But we shouldn't interrupt ourselves, as this verse by my sister points out:

One morning I woke and began resolutely
To work till my tasks were done absolutely.
I decided I would not waste even a minute—
In the race against time, I determined to win it.

I started all right, first clearing the dishes,
Then saw it was time to clean the bowl for the fishes.
As I reached for the cleanser, I thought that I'd better
Grab soap flakes as well for washing a sweater.

As I went for the sweater, I saw that the bed
Needed straightening, so stopped to do that instead.

Just then the phone rang, and while I was answering it,
I saw plants on the sill that needed watering a bit.

So went my day, and I worked till bone tired;
Then happy and proud, I sat back and admired.
But taking stock of my home, my joy soon diminished;
Everything was started, but nothing was finished.
                                        —Donette V. Ockey

4. Invest in proper tools.

I'm grateful to be alive during the permanent-press era, when it takes two minutes to iron a white shirt rather than twenty. I remember helping my mother do the wash when I was a little girl. I can still see the big double-tub washer she had to roll to the center of the room and slowly fill with water. I can still smell the starch bubbling on the stove, and I recall being amazed that bluing could make sheets whiter. A large, deep scar on my arm reminds me of an encounter with the wringer. It took my mother all of one day to do the laundry, then another full day to do the ironing. In today's world, no one should have to wash or iron all day, thanks to technological advances in equipment and improved fabrics.

Tools or equipment used in housekeeping can be categorized in three groups: large, medium, and small. Large tools include washers, dryers, dishwashers, self-cleaning ovens, frost-free refrigerators, freezers, microwave ovens, and trash compacters. These items are expensive; sometimes it requires years to purchase all of them. Some families have to do without some of them and manage beautifully anyway. Others prefer to do without because they're clinging to old habits and ways. (It's been said that a person's age can be determined by the degree of pain he or she feels when coming in contact with a new idea!) When used properly, however, these items become the servants of our generation.

Medium-size tools include vacuum cleaners, garbage disposers, bread mixers, food processors, blenders, toasters, waffle irons, electric hand mixers, electric skillets, irons, and crockpots. These items save time and improve the standard of our living.

The list of small tools is endless, and we all have things we "can't live without." These include quality cookware (pots, pans, baking sheets) on which food doesn't stick or burn. They include a variety of good knives, slicers, and scrapers, measuring cups and spoons, can openers, wire whisks, tongs, wooden spoons, spatulas, rubber scrapers, pastry blenders, hamburger presses, brushes, sponges, and cleaning agents. Canning kettles and accessories add to the safety as well as the efficiency of home canning. One could hardly imagine a carpenter with just a hammer or a surgeon with only a knife; we all need to be well equipped for the job.

Professional custodians can teach homemakers a great deal about how to do a job quickly and well. They recommend proper tools and equipment, the right cleaning solutions, and efficiency in approach and motion. For instance, a toilet bowl can be cleaned in seconds rather than minutes if done the professional way.

5. Dovetail — fit two tasks together.

It is sometimes possible and practical to do more than one thing at a time. With good planning you can accomplish some things that otherwise might not get done at all.

My favorite "doubling up" activity is to work quietly while I'm on the telephone. When the phone rings at our house or when I have calls to make, I go to either the kitchen or the laundry room, where I can keep busy sorting, spotting, folding, mending, and pressing while I telephone. Food preparation—cutting, peeling, and slicing—seems to take no time at all with a good friend at the other end of the line. Such tasks as baking cookies, rolling out pies, and forming bread dough go well with telephone calls. I set the table, load and unload the dishwasher, wipe off fingerprints, and manicure my nails while phoning. When my work is finished, I turn to an afghan I'm crocheting. One year I made three afghans while talking on the phone, which gives some insight into a Relief Society president's telephone time! Sometimes my calls are lengthy as people pour out their problems to me, and I listen better when my hands are busy. Also, it means a lot to me to know that even though I've had six phone calls in rapid succession, dinner will still be on time at our house.

Another good dovetailing trick is to prepare food in double or even triple portions and store or freeze part of it for use later. These time-free meals can do a lot to reduce pressure; it's encouraging on a busy day to have a casserole waiting in the freezer or a stew simmering in the crockpot. Many women who work outside the home claim that family life is immeasurably improved when they prepare meals ahead of time. Then they can return home from work to a dinner in the refrigerator or freezer waiting to be heated. While that food is cooking, they begin preparations for the next day's food. Thus dinner can often be ready within minutes from the time the first family member walks in the door and turns on the oven or the stove.

It's smart to stock up on homemade dry and moist mixes. In this way, 90 percent of the preparation is done in volume in advance, with only a quick 10 percent required at the last minute. By the way, volume cooking saves money, too.

Most people think ahead enough to run several errands each time they go out in the car, thus saving gasoline and time. But how many of us take advantage of this travel time by enjoying cassette tapes of inspirational talks, scriptures, great literature and music, or even language lessons? Such tapes can help transform routine travel into a stimulating educational experience, and they can also be used while we're doing our housework.

One parting word of caution: we need to avoid becoming too efficient. This key, along with the others, is helpful only in moderation. If carried to the extreme, it is no longer a true principle. To illustrate—a husband once complained that his wife was so efficient that he couldn't even get up at night for a drink of water without returning to find his bed made! Let's let our key to be efficient work *for* us, not against us.

Key 3

Do First Things First

An essential ingredient of effective management is a system for the routine part of housework. It is important to establish an order in which to do things, while also considering children's demands and the many interruptions that inevitably come along. I have found over the years that the order in which things are done is almost as important as whether they are done at all.

Managing a home can be compared to building a house that has a cornerstone, a foundation, and a structure. The cornerstone, so to speak, is usually Mother. If Mother looks all right and feels all right, everything in the house seems to function better. In most homes the mood of the day starts right there with her. As I see it, there are two dimensions to this cornerstone—the physical and the emotional and spiritual.

The first big step in mastering the physical dimension is to arise early. It is critical to the success of the day to get up and get going. Someone insightfully said that all too frequently there's nothing more exhausting than an extra hour's sleep.

After arising early, I find that the sooner I'm dressed, the more successful my day is. If I wander about the house in a flipping, flopping housecoat, wearing slippers that look like dead rabbits, I just don't do as well. It's easier to do the part when we look the part.

Beauty is a duty. It might be well for a woman to copy that slogan on paper and place it in the top drawer to be seen every morning as she dresses. It is vital that we take good care of ourselves, that we look our best. This reminds me of two men who had been friends but who hadn't seen each other for years. One day they happened to meet, and one asked the other if his wife were still as beautiful as ever. "Oh, yes," he replied, "she really is. Only it takes her a lot longer now."

Whatever it takes, it matters a great deal that we are as attractive as ever. A pleasing appearance does a lot for one's self-respect. It also means so much to a husband to be able to feel proud of his wife. She can really make him look good; his good taste and sharp judgment are reflected in her.y A mother's attractiveness does a lot for her children's attitudes, too. If she looks smart, she must be smart. On the other hand, if she looks dowdy, they might think she is dowdy. They could even regard her advice and counsel as such, and no one can afford this in today's world of sophisticated teenagers.

Just as with household furnishings and decor, good taste in clothing knows no price tag. It's not how much it costs or where we purchased it or even if we bought it at all, but how we put it together that makes us look attractive.

Most of us have learned the hard way that it can be a lot easier to keep weight off than it is to take it off. The value of good eating habits and proper exercise cannot be stressed enough. Here are two helpful exercises that everyone should do every day: push yourself away from the table and climb on the scales.

Just as important as the physical dimension is the emotional and spiritual side of the cornerstone. Just as our bodies need regular food and nourishment to keep them strong and well, so our spirits need to be fed daily to keep them healthy. Our spirits are best fed by prayer and daily scripture reading. Someone once explained to me that when we want to talk to the Lord we should pray, and when we want the Lord to talk to us we should read the scriptures.

I have been keeping a journal since I was eighteen. I've reached the point now where I could hardly live without it. I appreciate the emphasis President Spencer W. Kimball has placed on this. He has told us that journal writing will help keep us righteous. We have to live well in order to be able to report well. My journal helps me avoid the pileup in my life; it relieves stress and tension. I prefer putting the pressure on paper rather than on my mind. Journal keeping is therapeutic. It helps me live more deeply, fully, and meaningfully. It stimulates me to see stories and lessons and meanings in daily living. Some people miss a lot in life, like the man who left his car to look at the Grand Canyon, commented "Oh, that's a big hole," and returned to the parking lot. Recently I heard a woman sigh and say halfheartedly, "What a life. It's just been another ordinary day." She seemed so sorry. That night I wrote in my journal that I was grateful for an ordinary day— no one was hurt, no one became ill, everything went as planned and hoped for. Above all, a journal enables me to see the hand of the Lord in things I might have missed the first time around. As I live my life over again for the second time, so to speak, through writing a journal I see the blessings, the promptings, the answers, the miracles, the hand of the Lord. I marvel at the many minor miracles that make up my life. My journal helps me to be a much more grateful, faithful person.

This, then, is the cornerstone. I put it in place every day to help keep the structure of my life and of our home on the square. It seems to help hold everything else in place. Finding the time to do this is the challenge. It seems that the more one needs some peace and quiet, the less likely he or she is to get it. At one point we had six children, the oldest of whom was seven; later there were eight children twelve years old and under. Those were demanding years, when most of my time was taken up in the care of little mouths and bottoms. I always took care of the physical side of the cornerstone early every morning, but sometimes the emotional and spiritual part had to be strung out through the day. I snatched moments whenever possible to pray or read or write. Sometimes I met the challenge by arising earlier than usual, but that wasn't practical or wise when I'd already been up through the night with a teething baby. At other times the children's nap time (when I could get them all down at the same time) became my cornerstone time. Some days it was almost bedtime before I found a bit of time for myself.

A young mother told me that her husband, understanding the value of this private time in her life, gives her at least fifteen minutes every day and an hour or more on Sunday. He completely takes over the children and household. During that time, the children know to call Daddy rather than Mama. He and the children receive great dividends on this investment in his wife's interests.

Now, on to the foundation. Laying it is simply performing the basic, routine housework every morning. This includes making beds, hanging up nightclothes, polishing up in bathrooms, preparing school lunches, serving breakfast and cleaning up the kitchen, and caring for the children and supervising them in their activities and duties. This foundation work also includes some laundry. I prefer to do some washing every day—a batch of whites, one of semiwhites or coloreds, and one of easy-care, if necessary. This way the laundry never seems to take any time, and I can go after the spots and stains while they're fresh. In summary, the foundation work is just a quick pickup and wipe-off throughout the house. It's a skim job where I spend from two to five minutes in each room and from ten to twenty in the kitchen. (The children put their own rooms and bathrooms in order, and they also assist with some of the routine work.)

This surface tidying up should be accomplished between eight and ten every morning, depending on the ages and stages of the children. If the family is grown and away from home, a woman may be able to complete it by eight o'clock most mornings and then go on to other things. Caring for a new baby might extend this time to eleven or after. Sometime during those morning hours, however, a homemaker should have her house in order, and it is when her house is in order that her work really starts.

After the foundation is secure, we can begin our structure. We can build. It's amazing how high and how well we can build on the foundation of an orderly house. Building includes guiding and teaching our children. (Caring for them is foundation work.) It is a pity that sometimes parents are building and they don't seem to know it. They just think they are tending the children. If only they could realize that they are teaching and guiding and building—even for eternity—how much their perspective could change and how much greater would be their fulfillment!

Building also includes such things as housecleaning, cooking, baking, sewing, mending, gardening, decorating, and being involved in projects, errands, activities, service to the Church, community involvement, and personal and family development. The list is almost endless.

A common problem is that some homemakers never get to the building part. They are hung up on the routine. They rarely get past the point of making the beds, picking up the clutter, sweeping the crumbs, and on and on, over and over again, day after day. This is all they ever seem to do, and the situation gets to them eventually. They tell themselves that housework is futile because all they did today was what they did yesterday, and they're going to have to do it over again tomorrow. No wonder people are often attracted by influences outside the home, as they search for ways to better fulfill their lives. If only these unhappy homemakers could understand and apply the principles of good home management, they would pass the frustration level and move up to the fulfillment level of homemaking and find success and happiness there.

Other homemakers have trouble with this idea of a cornerstone, foundation, and structure because they are too thorough too soon. They cannot just wipe off a spot; they feel compelled to wash the entire wall. Washing the wall comes later; early in the morning we should just hit the spots. There are several reasons for this. First, we should quickly put our house in order everywhere to begin with so that it looks good.

No matter what happens or who comes to the door, we feel good about it. This does wonders for our attitude and our ambition, which are closely related. Everyone deserves a house that looks good, at least superficially. Second, this gives us control of things. If we're off washing a wall someplace when we should be quickly clearing up after breakfast, that's when little Johnny paints the kitchen with butter, dumps sugar in his hair, and lets the milk run down his ears. In most homes when things break, fall, or spill it's because they weren't where they belong. There is almost always an avoidable reason when things go wrong. Most bad days are of our own making. The control we get by first laying the foundation is practically priceless. So we shouldn't be too thorough too soon. In other words, smart home managers skim before they scour.

Some other homemakers have trouble with this concept of cornerstone, foundation, and structure because they try to skip the foundation. They attempt to build without it. They dive into their projects before the table is cleared, or the floor is swept, or the beds are made, and then wonder why everything crumbles and tumbles. Nothing seems to go right. One morning at about seven-thirty a woman was making the bed. Halfway through the job she noticed a clothes closet nearby that needed cleaning, so she left the bed partly done and began on the closet. She became so engrossed in its contents that she spent the rest of the day sorting things out. When her husband returned home from work about five-thirty, the children had been neglected, the house was in a shambles, the breakfast dishes were still on the table, their bed was only half-made, and there was his wife in her bathrobe in the clothes closet. He accused her of not getting anything done. She protested that she had been working hard—and she had, in the closet. If only she had turned the day around and had first dressed herself and cared for her children and put the house in order, and then worked in the closet, it would have been a wonderful day. A quick note about closets: if you allot eight hours for cleaning one, it will take eight hours. If you give four, it will require four. Projects always seem to absorb all the time we'll give them, so don't allot them more than they're worth.

All good home managers whom I've observed run their houses on a cornerstone, foundation, structure plan. Perhaps they don't understand the law that they're keeping, or they call it by another name, but they all consciously and subconsciously believe in putting their houses in order before going on to other duties. The basic concept is the same and the rewards are there for everyone.

It's almost always easier to do things right than to do them wrong. I've discovered the hard way that failing to lay the cornerstone and foundation demands too high a price. For instance, during the years when I was having babies and suffering from morning sickness, I learned it was better to force myself out of bed and almost crawl to the kitchen to prepare breakfast rather than to allow four preschoolers to fix their own. It's a lot smarter to be on the job and remove the clothing from the dryer on the last tumble than to allow the clothes to sit there wrinkling themselves so that they require ironing. Furthermore, if laundered clothing isn't folded and put away, it can be an even bigger job for us to try to find two stockings in the mound.

In all honesty, I must quickly admit that it isn't always this easy, nor does it work so well every single day. This is the ideal, something to work toward. As Robert Burns encouraged us, "A man's reach should exceed his grasp, else what's a heaven for?" I have had many, many mornings, especially when the children were young, when complications arose and the plan failed to materialize. Even now that the children are older and things move a lot more smoothly, things still can go awry. Perhaps a heavy snowfall during the night sends everyone outside with shovels to do our walks and leaves me inside with all my work and theirs in addition. Another day a car pool may fail and I might have to make an unscheduled drive to the high school, putting me behind a little in my work. This is life. It's part of the curriculum we have to take to prepare us for graduation. Sometimes when things are the worst, we learn and grow the most. So even though there are some days when this plan fails, it's worth it to keep trying, because there are many, many more days when it succeeds. When it does, the rewards are worth striving for.

As my husband and children return home from their work and school day, they're eager to find a happy wife and mother, a clean, neat house, and a good dinner. It doesn't seem to matter to them if it took me ten minutes or ten hours to get to that point. If I have gone shopping during the day or planted petunias or read part of a book or taught a class or given a lecture or run errands or spent the day in church service, they think, "Good for Mother! We're glad she had a nice day, too." If they should return home, however, to find me frustrated and frazzled, the house messy, and dinner starvation-style, they would resent anything I might have done during the day, and the last thing I want to have happen at our house is for my husband or children to withdraw their support and goodwill. Nor do I want the children to become resentful toward or lose interest in the things I believe to be all-important. Our eldest son made the rule that 50 percent of all that we cooked had to remain at home for the family to eat. Otherwise, he said, he was afraid he might smell cookies and not be able to find any. And that's not the way to help a growing boy like Relief Society!

I do not want to be known as a better church worker or neighbor than I am a wife, mother, and homemaker. I understand that if I am first the wife, mother, and homemaker, there is almost always time to be the other, but if I turn it around and serve others first, things run away from me and I fail to be where I'm needed most. I've found that the cornerstone, foundation, structure principle serves us well. There are occasions when emergencies arise in our neighborhood. At these times I drop anything and everything to help. When such a crisis comes along, my husband and children rally and do my work and theirs too, and they feel good about helping. But some people declare too many emergencies. They are the disasters themselves, and family members soon lose interest in helping.

Before leaving this chapter, I want to focus a little closer, to give a little more detail to the actual routine of managing the house. We'll talk about how I did it when our eight children were growing up and I was extremely involved with them and very much tied to the home. Then we'll discuss how I manage now, with half of the children married and the others away from home much of the day. Next we'll have a single parent tell us how he takes care of two children and the housework. And finally, a mother of nine children who was in bed for five months with mononucleosis will tell us what happened at her house during that time. Home management systems vary according to circumstances. The important thing is to have the right system for the right situation. (There are times when operating on a system of selected neglect might be the only way!)

Today, with only four children at home and much of my time devoted to activities and services outside the home, my system has been altered a little. There are more people to help now and fewer to mess up, so housework has been drastically reduced. Thus, every morning I put the house completely in order (and it usually remains that way all day!), and then I include some weekly duties, such as marketing and running errands on Fridays and cleaning (with help from the children, if they're available) on Saturdays. On the other days I take fifteen minutes or so to include an extra job, such as deep vacuuming of one room until every room in the house has been done, deep dusting of the rooms, washing windows outside, washing windows inside, polishing furniture, dusting plant leaves, cleaning bathroom tile, cleaning range top (ovens clean themselves), wiping out refrigerator and freezer, dusting wall hangings, dusting shutters and blinds, reorganizing closets or storage areas, and so forth.

With such a system, the house looks good all the time, yet

Suggested Schedule

Daily
Make beds
Clean up and sweep kitchen
Clean bathroom fixtures and floor
Wash and fold a batch or two
    of clothes
Take out trash
Pick up throughout house
Prepare meals
Care for and train children

Monday and Wednesday
Dust furniture throughout house
Dry-mop floors and vacuum
    where necessary
Shake scatter rugs
Iron and mend

Tuesday and Thursday
Bake
Personal time for appointments,
    visiting, special projects

Friday
Change linens on some of beds
Plan menus and shop

Saturday
(*Follow this schedule if you have
    some helpers; if not, schedule
    some of cleaning for another
    day*)
Change linens on rest of beds
Vacuum carpet and upholstered
    pieces
Dust
Water plants
Remove fingerprints around
    doorways and light switches

Mop kitchen and bathroom floors
Wax floors, if needed
Cook and bake for Sunday meals

Sunday
Attend church meetings
Read and study
Family hour

*Also include one of the following
each week:*

First Saturday:
Dust baseboards and
    window ledges

Second Saturday:
Thorough vacuuming of sofa and
    upholstered chairs; clean
    mirrors, picture frames, lamp
    shades, light bulbs

Third Saturday:
Wash windows, if necessary

Fourth Saturday:
Mop and wax all floors;
    wash scatter rugs

Fifth Saturday:
Clean closets, cupboards, and
    drawers as needed; special
    family outing or other activity

Quarterly
Polish furniture
Clean range and oven
Defrost (if necessary) and clean
    refrigerator
Sort seasonal clothing

Semiannual
Spring and fall housecleaning

I don't have to spend more than a few minutes a day to make it so.

The following example of a single parent and the challenges he faces is provided by Bonnie Ryan McCullough:

"Theoretically, the working parent should have less housework to do. While he or she is away at work, the house stays as is and there won't be as many messes made. This is true only when no one else is home. If the children leave for school after you depart and arrive home before you do, the parent's work multiplies. It is not the nature of children to notice things that need to be done or to carry out chores without adult supervision. The parent is likely to feel like a martyr who is slaving away to put bread on the table while the kids are loafing at home. For the working parent to get control at home, the trick is to keep up faithfully with minimum maintenance (pickup, meals, dishes, and laundry) and gain the children's cooperation.

"Let's look at Larry's family. Larry is a single parent with two children—a fifteen-year-old daughter and an eight-year-old son. Outsiders might assume that Larry could give the traditional 'mother' jobs to the girl, who is older. Not true. She cannot keep up in school, mature naturally, and also carry the burden of keeping up a home. He cannot delegate the home responsibility so easily.

"Larry also carries an unpleasant memory of his working mother. After she started working, weekends were miserable because of her pushing and yelling at the family to finish all the cleaning, scrubbing, washing, ironing, baking, and yard work that she had previously been able to do during the week as a full-time homemaker. Not wanting this atmosphere to dominate his home, Larry made an effort to change in three ways. First, he relaxed the level of housekeeping; second, he set up a program of minimum maintenance; and third, he involved the children.

"Though he was relaxing the standard, he didn't accept clutter or filth. He gave up daily dusting for a more thorough dusting on Saturday. Because he kept up with the pickup, each room needed a thorough cleaning only every month or two. Painstakingly, Larry went through his home eliminating time-taking extras, storing a few treasures and getting rid of the rest. He created a place for everything, making the up-keep much easier.

"This father gets his children up with him at six o'clock. They all dress, eat together, and do a quick pickup through the house. When Larry leaves for work at seven-thirty, the morning routine is finished. Although the girl is to see the boy off to school, she has been spared breakfast preparation, cleanup, and disciplining her brother through his chores. Even though this first hour of the day is concentrated work, it leaves everyone free until dinnertime.

"When he delegated duties to the children, Larry eliminated confusion by specifying who, what, when, and how. Then he asked for feedback: 'What is your assignment?' He also knows that if the job is important enough to be assigned, it deserves parental inspection. Avoiding the army-sergeant technique, Larry tries to foster a feeling of teamwork and love. By nature, children do not see things that need to be done, and if the job isn't theirs, they feel no obligation. Even many adults haven't learned this yet—just ask any employer. Be patient with children.

"How does Larry handle dinner? We might assume, because he is a man, that he would rely on his daughter, but this family does the meal preparation together between five and six o'clock. Saturday morning they plan the weekly menus, trying to keep them simple but nutritious. The menus for the week are then posted so everyone understands which ingredients are for meals and which foods can be eaten for snacks.

"Rather than plan a strict schedule of duties, Larry leaves his evenings open for the activities and needs of his children and himself. Because they have worked together to keep things put away, the rooms are quite free from clutter. On Saturday morning they clean one room thoroughly. The rest of the weekend is saved for individual fulfillment or family fun—they all deserve it!

"Even though Larry is a single parent, his technique of planning and minimum maintenance can be applied with equal success to families in which both parents work." (Bonnie Runyan McCullough, *Bonnie's Household Organizer*, New York: St. Martin's Press. Used with permission.)

Finally, we come to the example of the temporarily disabled mother. Catherine was stricken with mononucleosis and was bedridden for three months and down part of the time for an additional two months. Due to demanding professional and Church responsibilities, her husband had limited time at home. They had nine children, ranging in age from eighteen years to a toddler.

Fortunately, the children had been well trained prior to their mother's illness, and they were in the habit of keeping their rooms in order and doing weekly chores such as cleaning the bathrooms, the family room, and the living and dining rooms.

In addition to this, the children over ten were given the responsibility of doing their own laundry, with emphasis on adding to their batch some of the younger children's clothing and household items. The children who could drive chauffeured the other children before and after school.

Each of the older children was assigned, on a rotation basis, to plan the evening meal, do the shopping, prepare the dinner, and clean up the kitchen. They were allowed full license in their menu selection. They appreciated this challenge, and there was a built-in control gauge. If a child served hot dogs too many times or presented an unsatisfying meal, he or she would hear about it from the other children. Paper plates and some disposable utensils were used, to keep cleanup to a minimum so the children could also handle their school work, practice their music, and participate in social and sports activities.

The parents wisely believed that the children should be allowed as much initiative and opportunity as they were assigned responsibility. This was undoubtedly a major key to the success of the situation.

Thoughtful extended family members, neighbors, and friends tended the preschoolers during the day, helped with car pooling, and brought in occasional dinners. The family felt that they never lost their dignity and that they didn't overburden anyone. The children learned the valuable lesson of being able to graciously and gratefully receive.

During this time Catherine, the mother, says she specialized in thank-yous. This became a creative act for her as she discovered new and different ways to express appreciation. While she was in bed those many weeks, she used her mind to develop ways to say thanks and to compose meaningful letters to give to her family. In addition to the positive effect these expressions of gratitude had on her husband and children, she found this a very healthy emotional outlet. She was doing something, rather than just lying in bed filled with guilt or self-pity.

There were compensations and blessings—there always are, if we live for them and look for them. Even though the mother was not allowed visitors or phone calls, she was always available to the children. She spent countless hours with them on a one-to-one basis or with several at a time. Together they read dozens of books. It was a unifying, loving time. Many lessons were learned. Personal discipline was sharpened. Priorities were sifted. There was great growth and gain for everyone. Now, several years later, it is proving to be a sweet memory.

As these examples illustrate, many different circumstances and life-styles can affect home management. But the cornerstone, foundation, structure concept remains important, and homemakers who learn to put first things first will find that the things that matter most will generally get done.

going to do in the morning, I sleep well and am motivated to arise on time. Crossing off items on the list is a fantastic tranquilizer. It's done! I can then relax, play, sleep, or whatever else I wish to do. Working with lists is therapeutic for me. And I'm sure that our Father in heaven is pleased with us when we learn to motivate ourselves naturally and to calm ourselves naturally. Lists do that for me.

The story is told of a woman who was crossing her list off one evening when she realized she had done some things that were not on the list, so she quickly wrote them down just to cross them off. It's good to give ourselves such a reward.

We should make certain, however, that our lists help us rather than hinder us. A person should not go to bed some night feeling sorry for herself because she did only eight out of ten things. We need to think of what we did accomplish rather than what we did not. We shouldn't allow a super day to be spoiled because we didn't get everything done—probably no one could have. Duties undone can be transferred to tomorrow's list. If we focus on what we did do, and treat our-

selves to a positive attitude, we'll have more energy to get going again the next day.

One woman told her friend that she had good news and bad news. The good news was that she had just completed her "to do" list. The bad news was that it was yesterday's list. Actually, this usually doesn't even matter, as long as the jobs get done. I make lots of lists with no dates or times indicated. I just work down the list as I'm able to, and when one has been completed, I make another one. It's the progress and accomplishment, not the date, that usually matters in the long run.

Unfortunately, there's no magic in lists. They work only when we do. They are only as good as our own self-discipline and motivation are—and those are things we ourselves have to supply.

Besides my to-do lists, a type of list that I really rely on is my grocery list. I start with a piece of typing paper folded in six columns. (Folding paper is a smart, quick way to organize.) The columns are labeled as follows: Produce, Meats, Miscellaneous, Utility, Frozen, and Other. "Other" means things I buy other than at the grocery store, such as at the post office or hardware store. As I add to the list during the week, it automatically organizes itself. The columns also fit aisles in the supermarkets where I shop. Making a list helps me to shop quickly and efficiently, to avoid buying too much or not enough, and to control impulse purchases. Because of it, I rarely forget items I need. I keep the paper folded in my hand as I shop so as to not appear too conspicuous. Once a month I shop heavily to restock our food supply. Other weeks I purchase only perishables and ingredients for specific recipes. Frequently one or two of our children will accompany me to the store, and I'll divide the list, giving each of them a column or two. With such teamwork, the shopping is quickly done.

One common problem with list making is expressed in this little verse:

My husband, with his day's work done,
Says, "You should organize;
Be more efficient in your work;
Make plans, dear, visualize!"

I try to follow his advice,
I schedule—he insists,
And I could be efficient, too,
If I could just *find* my lists!

Often a person will say, "Oh, where did that piece of paper go? I had something important written on it," or, "Who threw away that envelope? I had a note on the back of it." Another typical comment is, "Oh, I had it written down, but I forgot to look at my list."

We can easily avoid such problems by using a notebook for our lists and making it an integral part of our life.

I discovered my notebook years ago when I was a missionary in Holland. (My particular notebook is a loose-leaf style, about three by five inches in size. There are other types of good agenda books on the market; the important thing is to have one.) I fell in love with it immediately, and it's been my constant companion ever since. If I lost it, I'm afraid I would collapse. I would have to go to bed and stay there! I keep my little book near the main telephone of the house and refer to it all day long. Then it goes with me in my purse along with my car keys and driver's license. The only time I don't carry it is when I'm out socially. Then I'm off duty.

Let me give you a quick tour through my notebook so you can see how it serves me. Inside the front cover is a pocket where I keep "floating" slips of paper, such as claim checks from the dry cleaners or the shoe repair shop. I also keep my grocery list there. I used to make my list on one of the pages of the book, but our family has outgrown that. I'm no longer just a shopper—I'm a purchasing agent!

My notebook then begins with a page for identification, a page for the current year's calendar, and one for last year's and next year's. I also keep a page in the front for listing personal, family, and household goals. Because the notebook is loose-leaf style, I can add or subtract pages or rearrange them to suit my style.

Next there is a page for each day. On the left side of the page, the hours of the day are listed. Here I jot down specific appointments I have, such as a meeting at ten o'clock, a child's music lesson at four-thirty, a wedding reception at eight. In this column I also list the menu for the evening

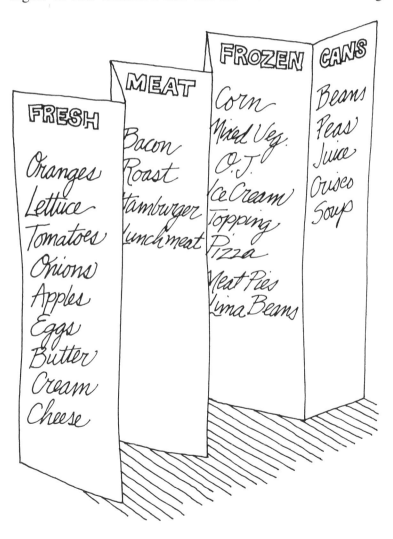

meal. I plan my menus in advance when I make out my grocery list for the week. In this way, I know all week long what we're going to eat each day. I can switch menus around, of course, but at least the plans have been made and the ingredients are on hand. This helps me to be a happy second-mile cook rather than a desperate first-mile one. When you feed ten people every meal, you can't just throw something together and please the crowd. It's important to have something steaming, soaking, thawing, raising, setting up, or whatever. Besides, in meal planning, as with many other things, once you have the idea, the job is half-done.

On the right side of the page is my to-do list. Here I write down the things I need to do, in order of their importance. As a young bride I listed such things as making beds, doing dishes, and peeling potatoes, but I got over that about the second day. Now I just list the things beyond the routine: the special projects, the phone calls, the errands, and so forth. And these are the satisfying items to cross off.

The lists in my little notebook serve me in another way that is quite sacred to me. I find that when I write down the things I know I need to do, the things I didn't know I needed to do are made known to me. With my mind clear due to the list, I am receptive to promptings and nudgings by the Spirit, and wonderful things happen.

My notebook is even helpful in my personal relationships. Whenever someone tells me that something is anticipated, such as a doctor's appointment for some tests or word about a hoped-for promotion, I make a note and check with the person later to see how things turned out. This pleases my friends, and it brings me satisfaction. I'm interested in many people, and this is the best way for me to show my interest and concern. If I keep too much on my mind, I overload the circuit, so to speak, and information starts bouncing off. Our minds were not intended to be filing cabinets. My notebook helps me to keep mine clear so that I can be alert to new situations and respond accordingly.

I carry two months' worth of daily pages in my notebook:

the current month and one month in advance. I also carry a full year's worth of "month-at-a-glance" pages for long-range planning. If the dentist wants to see me in six months, I can list it. If I'm interested in doing a project but it's June and I know I can't get to it until the children return to school, I jot it down for September. Just putting it on paper eases the frustration I might otherwise feel from having more ideas than time.

My notebook also contains sections for finances, for addresses and phone numbers, and for other miscellaneous notes. I have one page where I list clothing sizes and other pertinent information that's handy to have when I'm out shopping. On another page I list my housecleaning schedule. Then there is a page for Hank, one for me, and one for each of our children, and on these pages are our wish lists. I write down things each person might like to have sometime, such as for Christmas, birthdays, or Father's Day. I can't remember these good ideas ten months later; in fact, I can't even remember them three days later. Someone said, "Ideas are like birds. They fly in and right out again unless you catch and cage them." This book cages my ideas.

I keep a page for good ideas to be used in connection with my church assignments. I have a page of ideas for family home evenings and Sunday family times. If a child asks a question, or we see a need in the family, or there's an article we'd like to share, or I think of a concept that needs teaching, or there's a place we'd like to go, I note it. These ideas surely improve the quality of our church service as well as our family time.

On another page I list ideas I might use to develop into magazine articles or talks or lessons. Ideas come at odd moments; if I list them as I think of them I can always develop them later. When sons or daughters are away at school or on missions, I keep notes of interesting items to include in letters and phone calls. I also carry a supply of blank pages for copying recipes or perhaps a profound thought by a speaker in church.

I believe that the most important feature of the notebook is that I can carry it with me. No matter where I am, I can make a commitment, jot down a note, or whatever. This eliminates unnecessary phone calls and chances of forgetting. If something is written down, I'll follow through.

My little brown notebook is one of my most valuable possessions because it makes everything else function in my life. It is a major help in everything I do. It is more than an appointment book—it is a way of life.

Ralph Waldo Emerson once said that everyone should carry with him two books, one to read in and the other to write in. And, I might add, to dream in. We can get things done and dreams can come true when we plan ahead, have a flexible schedule, and develop the notebook habit.

Key 5

Enlist the Family's Cooperation

One day when I answered our telephone, an irate voice on the other end demanded, "Are you the lady who wrote that book?"

I prepared to defend myself, gulped, and said, "Yes."

She hurried on, almost in a scream: "I just want to tell you that before you can run a perfect house, you've got to have a perfect husband. And when you get the answer to that, let me know!" With that, she banged the receiver down.

Needless to say, homemaking and child rearing go a lot smoother if there is team effort on the part of husband and wife. Family living can be much more rewarding and successful if both partners are supportive of one another and are united in their goals and willing to work together to attain them.

To me, the ideal marriage is one in which each partner does everything possible for the happiness of his or her spouse. If something matters to one, it should matter to the other.

A beautiful marriage is based on the desire of two people to bring out the best in one another. They have entered marriage with preparations and expectations for success. It is said that the loveliest words Sir Winston Churchill ever penned were those he wrote in the church registry on the day of his marriage: "In September 1908 I married and lived happily ever after."

It is not my intent to discuss a husband's and a wife's responsibilities in providing for the spiritual, physical, emo-

49

tional, and social welfare of their family. This is an individual arrangement and should be handled according to the circumstances in each home. But there are certain ways that they can work together at supporting each other, and these ideas might generate some creative thinking to help boost a partnership.

I believe that it is essential for a wife to assist her husband in providing for the family. Some women find it is necessary for them to work outside the home for additional income. Other women find that they can serve their families most effectively by remaining home and managing well. My neighbor commented that she could stay home and save more money than she could go out and earn. In making this decision, there is much to consider besides the dollar and cents aspect.

I once read a clever magazine article about how to marry the man with the most money. The answer: learn to make the most of your man's money. In other words, be a smart consumer so your money will go as far as possible. Avoid waste. (President Brigham Young said that some women can throw more out the back door with a teaspoon than their husbands can bring in the front door with a wheelbarrow.) Practice the "make, grow, and repair it yourself" theory with everything from clothing to bread. Cultivate a garden and can, freeze, or dry fruits and vegetables. Keep the mending up to date. Know how to remake and be creative with home furnishings so your house can be attractive without being unnecessarily expensive. Work as a family to prevent letting things around the home and yard become run down. If a piece of tile comes loose in the bathroom, repair it promptly before all the pieces around it fall off too. If a seam in the carpet is coming unstitched, mend it quickly before someone's toe snags it and tears up the carpet. If a slat in the fence falls out, put it right back. You can look and even feel financially successful by dressing yourself and your children nicely and keeping up your home. Looking attractive is more a matter of pride, ambition, and resourcefulness than it is of income.

A wife and husband should work together in putting their economic house in order. They should avoid overextending themselves. They should try to live within their means and build up a substantial reserve in savings. During times of plenty, they should heed the counsel of Church leaders and put away in their homes a storehouse of clothing and food.

Above all, a husband and wife should strive together to be worthy of the blessings and promises of the Lord in material matters as well as spiritual. The scriptures make it evident that He wants us to be prosperous and that He promises us this blessing through our faithfulness: "Prove me now herewith, saith the Lord of hosts, if I will not open you the windows of heaven, and pour you out a blessing, that there shall not be room enough to receive it." (Malachi 3:10.)

Remember that prosperity cannot always be measured by income. Sometimes the Lord blesses and helps his faithful servants to prosper indirectly, perhaps through increased opportunities, additional advantages, extra strength and ambition, more positive attitudes, or fewer problems and expenses. Latter-day leaders of the Church urge us to reflect the spirit of the gospel by being progressive and industrious. Laziness, carelessness, and slothfulness have no part in the gospel plan. Furthermore, misdirected values and selfishness that detract from our families and homes are not in keeping with the gospel.

As husbands and wives, we must learn the will of the Lord concerning those who keep His commandments, and then we must have faith in His promises and work to make them come true.

Yes, it does take a practically perfect husband (as well as a practically perfect wife) to make a practically perfect home. This probably won't happen the first year—maybe not even during the first ten or twenty or fifty years. It may take a lifetime and then some. But it is the direction, not just the destination, that counts.

Once a couple are working together, the next step is to enlist the cooperation of the children. One homemaker cried,

"All hands on deck or mother will sink." That's true—we do need the help! There is no way for parents to do the job alone. Furthermore, children need the development and training that come from well-defined and consistently assigned duties in the home. I believe that the home is the university for all eternity, the workshop of the Lord. It should be the best of all apprentice shops. There are some attitudes, habits, skills, and values to be learned at home that cannot be learned as well any other place.

When children grow up with good habits, they become strong and self-disciplined. As they acquire skills, they grow in confidence and competence. These strengths help give them self-respect. Children who feel good about themselves in turn feel good about everyone and everything else. They love and obey the Lord, their parents, and other authority figures in their lives. Their attitudes are healthy; their values are sound. Such children are cooperative and helpful in the home. With a little direction, effective family teams can be organized. The best families work together and then play and grow together. Some basic concepts can help us build such effective family relationships.

1. Learn to work together as a team.

When the house is pleasant and homey and good dinners and good times come along regularly, lots of help and cooperation are likely to occur. But if the house runs on crisis management and everything is chaotic, cluttered, and confused, all the helpers disappear. Who wants to be caught in such a mess? It is ironic but true that the more you look like you need help, the less likely it is that you will get it.

A child is much more likely to be interested in baking a cake if the kitchen has been cleared of the last meal. A child is much more willing to dust if the dining room table has just a centerpiece on it rather than the week's accumulation of papers, packages, and purses. Family members are much more willing to keep up with the repair work around the house if hammers and screwdrivers can be located easily.

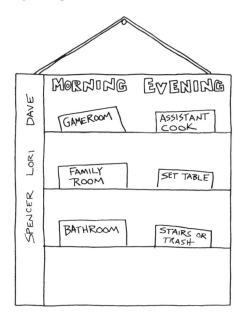

2. Be consistent and firm.

There is a power in consistency, with the pattern established, the expectations clear, and your mind made up. If you're inconsistent, however—if you asked your children to help yesterday and forgot about it today—next time you ask them they may try to talk you out of it.

Where chores are concerned, firmness means that the child doesn't quit until the job is done. We have stood fast by such rules as these: "When your room is in order, you may go out to play or leave for school." "The story will begin as soon as you put the toys away." "You may play ball as soon as you have finished practicing the piano."

To enforce this, I have occasionally had to go to school or wherever the child was and bring him or her home to complete the work. It generally takes just once! I don't bring the child home just because I want the bed made; I do it to teach a principle. This type of action is easier on everyone than are reminding, scolding, nagging, and threatening. (Where school is concerned, it seems that when a child toes the mark at home, he does well in his studies too.) A child who gains mastery over little things will have control over greater things.

Some parents I know once drove over a hundred miles round trip to bring home a teenage son who had lied to them. He didn't lie again. Some other parents drove almost nonstop from southern Texas to Rexburg, Idaho, to talk to a daughter at Ricks College who was doing some things she shouldn't. The trip made all the difference.

Child guidance experts tell us that it doesn't seem to matter what techniques parents use in rearing their children. Some parents raise their children by the book, and still the children turn out poorly. Other parents don't read the books and make every blunder, but their children do well. What counts in most cases is not the parenting skills or styles, but how much the parents care. Parents who inconvenience themselves for the good of their children evidently care.

There are many ways to be firm and to say "I care." They don't always have to be as drastic as the foregoing examples!

3. Be fair.

There are many applications of the concept of fairness. To begin with, avoid painting yourself into a corner. Give your children rules and reasons that you can live with, that can pass the test of time. Some parents fail to do this. Once one of our younger boys told me that his best friend received a quarter every time he made his bed. My son's questioning eyes told me he wondered why he didn't get paid for making his bed. Well, the reason he wasn't paid was because we were afraid that if we paid him a quarter to make his bed when he was eight, we wouldn't be able to afford him when he was eighteen. Instead, we prefer another reason for making beds or for doing other chores, a reason that will always be good— and that is, because you're supposed to. We give each of our children a small cash allowance until they are grown old enough to earn money through paper routes, baby-sitting jobs, or similar work, but there are no strings attached to it. The allowance has nothing to do with their behavior or services. There are better ways to handle such problems than through money. Experts say that if we are to teach our children sound money values, money should be a teaching tool rather than a punishment or a reward. It should be used to teach a child how to budget, save, and spend wisely. Of course, there are situations when some behavior modification—bribery, if you will—can be most useful, but not on a daily basis.

4. Make it fun and easy.

Incentive programs, games, and charts can be motivating and can also serve to make helping with household chores a positive, rather than a negative, experience, until the children become mature enough to be self-motivated. Here are some ideas for starters:

Let a child wear a little hand puppet (made from a sock or paper bag) as he picks up his toys. Allow him to tell the puppet what to do. This is a pleasant change from having an adult tell him what to do.

At bedtime one father plays army with his two little boys. He assigns them a rank and has them march and drill; before the children realize what's happened, they've picked up their playthings, put on their nightclothes, and paraded off to bed. (The amazing thing about this approach is that it actually requires less time than is involved in the usual going-to-bed struggle.)

Let the child pretend he is a taxi. Call for the "taxi." Let it zoom up to you; then send it on an errand, and let it zoom away. Three-year-olds love this.

Play a music box or recording or set the oven timer and challenge the children to complete a certain task before the music stops or the buzzer rings. This helps eliminate dawdling and the seemingly endless nature of a task.

Pretend to wind the children up like a toy as they begin a task. Children will actually come back to be rewound for the next job!

Children who are a bit older and who have a sense of humor respond to notes such as this: "You don't have to milk

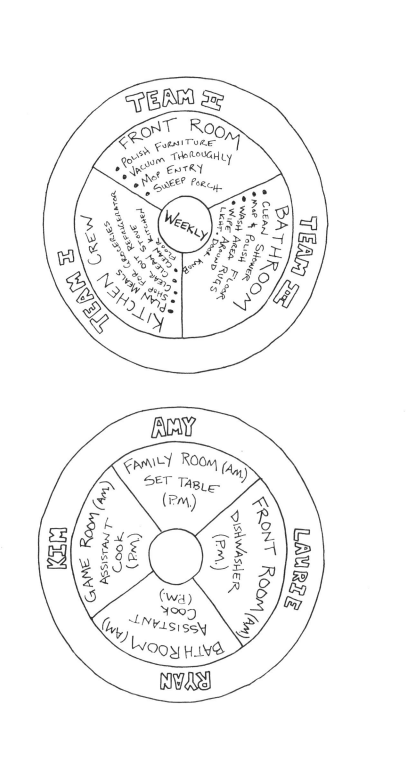

forty cows, the beets do not need thinning, the hay doesn't have to be stacked, the corral fence does not need mending, but will you please carry out the garbage." (This, of course, is for city children who would be intrigued by such overwhelming farm chores.)

Assign the child to be a certain animal (rabbit, dog, bird, and so on) and let him pretend to act like this animal as he performs assigned tasks.

When the children balk about picking up their toys, play "hidey tidey." One child leaves the room while the others pick up a few toys. The child returns and tries to guess what was picked up. The process is repeated until all the toys are put away.

Exchange roles, with a child acting as "mother" and directing the work activities.

Help children learn to dust thoroughly by playing "hidden treasures." Once a month or so, mother hides pennies under some of the vases, lamps, and bric-a-brac in the home. She can determine how well the children dust by how many pennies or "hidden treasures" were found.

A choice between two "yeses" is much better than a choice between a "yes" and a "no." For instance, instead of saying to a child, "Please take this to the clothes chute," and having him respond, "I don't want to," you might say, "I need two things done. Which would you prefer helping with—taking this to the clothes chute or running this out to the garage?" Usually a child responds by accepting one or the other assignment. Most children will help willingly if they are allowed to do some of their own thinking and decision making. What they resent is someone giving them orders all the time.

A game that never seems to grow old and even appeals to grown children is "twenty-pick-up." Perhaps a room is cluttered with toys, books, or papers. Call the children together and ask them each to pick up and put away twenty things, or whatever number of items appears necessary. Then watch the clutter disappear! Through such a game the children see both the beginning and the end of their task, which is very encouraging, and they don't have to worry whether or not others in the family are doing their part. Try this game next time your home or yard is cluttered or when there are weeds to pull or someone drops the can of crayons.

Assigning titles to work assignments can make work fun, such as Dust Deputy, Kitchen Katie, Bathroom Butch, or Parlor Polly. For example, Jolly Jump-Up serves during meals and answers the telephone or doorbell. Snappy Scraper scrapes and stacks the dishes. Wow-of-a-Washer loads the dishwasher or washes the dishes. Pert Polisher wipes off the kitchen table, chairs, countertops, range, and refrigerator. Emergency Ellen or Ed steps in to help if one of the others is not home.

5. Build and bless the child.

In addition to getting the job done, give the child ample portions of the following:

Attention. A child will do almost everything for a pay-off. Children crave recognition and attention. Reinforce the good that they do by noticing it (in a variety of creative ways), and eliminate the bad by ignoring it as far as possible.

Availability. This is more an attitude than an act.

Acceptance. Only in a climate of acceptance can a child grow and blossom.

Appreciation. This is the pay that life runs on.

Advantages. As we endeavor to give our children all the advantages that we didn't have, let's remember to give them the ones we did have.

Affection. This is as essential to the development of children as are food and sunshine.

A good home is like an apprentice shop where everything is passed on, side by side, hand over hand—from living and loving to working and worshipping. This demands a lot from parents, but it is truly worth it. A few headaches when children are young can save heartaches when they're grown up.

Key 6

Be of Good Cheer

Throughout this book a lot has been said about habits that build us through personal discipline and that in turn help our homes through effective management. One of the most important habits that can be developed is that of attitude. Having a habit of being of good cheer can make a wonderful difference in our lives. I believe that being happy or not being happy is greatly a matter of habit. Abraham Lincoln showed this insight into human nature when he said, "Most men [and women] are about as happy as they make up their minds to be."

It is easy to slip into a habit of being unhappy. A woman can be completely unaware that she has become caught up in the trap of murmuring, complaining, and criticizing. She might not even realize that she has allowed a negative, self-defeating pattern to develop in her life. As she continually poisons her system with negative feelings, she can make herself emotionally or physically ill—or both. Medical science is constantly learning about psychosomatic diseases and what a tremendous effect the mind can have on the body. Many illnesses and physical problems are triggered by negative emotional responses and stress.

Husbands and family members often suffer, too. An old verse reads:

> Three things drive a man from home:
> A house that reeks,
> A roof that leaks,
> And a woman who scolds whenever she speaks.

There's a similar warning in Proverbs: "It is better to dwell in a corner of the housetop, than with a brawling woman in a wide house." (Proverbs 21:9.)

Every mother knows that it is largely her role to determine the emotional climate of the household. She can do much to keep things sunny and warm and pleasant. As the adversary tries to thwart the work of the Lord today by destroying eternal families, his target is frequently the woman. Satan seems to know that if he can get the mother on his side, he can usually conquer the whole family. Therefore, he is in search of a woman's Achilles' heel, and when he finds it, he tries to destroy her through restlessness, discontent, discouragement, depression, or whatever gets her down. He isn't often able to influence Latter-day Saint women through alcohol, drugs, or immorality, so he works on their attitudes and all too frequently gets them there. Discouragement is the tool that he reserves for the righteous.

Many of my acquaintances suffer from chronic discouragement or varying degrees of depression. Much of my mail and many of my telephone conversations deal with those types of problems. I believe the reason depression seems to be prevalent among Latter-day Saint women is that when it strikes, we feel so guilty about it that we compound the problem. Also, we're so closely knit as a group that many people are aware of our problems.

What amazes me is that usually there is little correlation in a person's life between her problems and her degree of happiness. It all goes back to one's inner feelings about oneself, not to outward circumstances. We all know of people who have real trials and serious problems to face, yet who make the most of each situation and avoid making two problems out of one. Some people can be happy and optimistic regardless of their circumstances. A beautiful example of this comes from the diary of Eliza R. Snow. Her writings revealed the many miseries of crossing the plains, and yet she recorded, "Surely happiness is not dependent on circumstances."

On the other hand, the person who seems to have everything going for her is often one who struggles with negative feelings and discouragement and depression. Is it possible that life can be too easy? I've heard that we can dodge the elephants; it's the gnats that get us down!

We achieve an exciting breakthrough in personal understanding when we learn that even though we cannot always choose what happens to us, we can choose our own response to it. Each one of us must decide if we are going to act or react in a situation, and just how we are going to do it.

Some forms of depression—those which are diagnosed as being clinical—do require expert medical help to overcome. They are actually illnesses and have to be treated as such. Therapy, such as drugs and diet, can help toward recovery. Depression of this nature is a gravely serious problem and needs immediate attention. It is critical for husbands and other family members to understand this and to help the woman get the medical attention she so desperately needs.

Other forms of discouragement and depression, however, can often be overcome by a woman's declaring, "Get thee behind me, Satan," and determining to buck up and get hold of herself. Through prayer, fasting, and effective counseling with her priesthood leaders—her husband, her home teachers, and her bishop—and through taking some constructive steps to mend her negative feelings and build positive ones, she can usually work herself out of the problem. This requires a great deal of inner strength, determination, and faith, and outward encouragement and support, but the problem can usually be solved. Following are a few suggestions for overcoming depression and being of good cheer.

1. Start a self-improvement program.

Many helpful articles and books on depression are available. One of the most helpful of these books, and one that I'd like to recommend to men and women everywhere, is Dr. James Dobson's *What Wives Wish Their Husbands Knew*

About Women. Dr. Dobson points out that most depression results from low self-esteem and feelings of inadequacy and inferiority. Therefore, a constructive step in feeling better about oneself is to embark upon a self-improvement program. Of course, this can be a difficult assignment, but it can be done. I know dozens of heartening success stories. A woman can build her self-esteem by increasing her knowledge or skills in some area. A word of caution, however: She must take it a step at a time, one project before another. No one can get there in one big bound. But working to improve oneself can make all the difference in a woman's self-esteem.

Many books and classes and courses are available that can supplement every woman's personal efforts to grow, improve, and overcome. Then, after she has learned to do well the required things in her life, she can specialize. She can learn to do one thing exceptionally well, or learn all she can about a specific subject, such as tole painting, gardening, baking, giving book reviews, music, tennis, writing, or Greek or Chinese cookery. She might also become an authority on a subject, such as nineteenth-century literature, Church history, or a principle of the gospel.

It is important that a woman have an identity of her own, beyond that of being a wife and mother. It is essential for her well-being that she have some victories of her own, including some outside her role in the home. The Church and community provide many opportunities for this dimension of life, and it can be pursued within the framework of the gospel and with the Lord's blessings. It is important to increase in ability, knowledge, and service. A growing person is one who is more likely to find life challenging and rewarding.

2. Find joy in simple things.

People who seek pleasure in simple things often find it easier to live above depression than do those whose lives are cluttered and complicated. It is important to enjoy and appreciate autumn leaves, sunsets, the tide roaring in, falling snow, flowers blooming, kittens at play, white fluffy clouds, a flitting butterfly, lilacs on a bush, a polished floor, white ruffled curtains at a sparkling window, a log burning on the hearth, a well-tended garden, the patter of rain on a roof, the aroma of bread baking, the softness of a newborn baby, a good book, and a quiet evening.

3. Be in good physical shape.

Doctors report that people who are in excellent physical condition rarely suffer from emotional fatigue. Tests have shown that some elements in the body that tend to tear it down and that are produced by anxiety and stress can be removed by regular daily exercise. It is difficult to sustain a state of depression when one's heart rate is increased through brisk walking, jogging, swimming, bicycling, or other aerobic exercise.

4. Avoid comparing yourself with others.

One of the most destructive things that threaten attitude is to make comparisons of oneself with others. Too often a person will compare the worst of herself to the best of others. Or she will assume things that aren't really so at all. I was at the hairdresser's one day when a woman came in who had the longest, thickest, darkest, most gorgeous hair I've ever seen. She was to have her hair styled for an advertisement for designer jeans. As we talked, she explained that only her hair would be in the ad; the photographer would use someone else's face, a third person's body, and a fourth person's legs. A total of four women would make up that photograph—a picture of a woman who didn't really exist! Yet, not knowing this, every woman who sees the ad will measure herself against the picture and perhaps feel inferior because she doesn't look like that.

Making comparisons for the sake of comparing is a self-defeating behavior pattern. We can always find someone who is better off and someone who is worse off than we are. The only valid, healthy comparison is with ourselves—just doing a bit better than we did yesterday.

Elsie May Smithies has said: "Naturally, it is a painful thing to have others know about our conflicts. I look at you and I see the nice clothes you have on. I look at myself and I know that the lining of my coat is torn. I don't know about your linings, but I do know about mine. You keep me from seeing yours and I keep you from seeing mine. But all the time I know about mine. I have to put what I know about myself outside and inside up against what I know about you outside only. The result is that I don't even suspect you of torn linings and worn out underclothes and I feel hurt about what is under my surface. The trouble is, we measure other people by what we see, ourselves by what we feel. None of us accepts this hurt complacently." We need to stop wasting energy wondering how things are with someone else. The only person to compete with is oneself; the only record to improve is one's own.

5. Do something for someone else.

At the grocery store one day I met a neighbor who was buying several bunches of daffodils. She explained that it was her birthday, and she was celebrating the day by taking flowers to some of her friends. Later that day, as a daffodil and a thoughtful note appeared on our porch, I was warmed by the gesture and impressed to see a woman so busy reaching out that she had no time to mourn growing a year older or to wish someone were doing something for her.

Being of good cheer has just two requirements: *reach out* and *reach up*.

As we *reach out*, we must first extend ourselves to our families. Samuel Johnson said, "The result of all ambition is to be happy at home." I know—and there are many stories to substantiate this—that when a woman is happy at home, generations are blessed. And when she is not happy at home, generations pay the price.

Realizing that I am a homemaker by divine appointment, that I am doing the task I was created to do, helps me to be happy at home. I've learned that skills bring thrills. I've learned that through adequate know-how, homemaking can bring fulfillment rather than frustration. And through effective management, there can be time left for myself and for some outside activities.

This is not to imply, however, that every moment of my motherhood has been glorious and joyful. It has not. You cannot rear eight children without having times when you'd sell them all for half price. I have sometimes felt overworked and overwhelmed. I have been so tired that I have cried. There were days during pregnancies when even a single batch of dirty dishes was too much to face. I have despaired over children and know how it feels to think you are an absolute failure. Now I can laugh about some of these situations; many of the trials of parenthood and the tricks of children provide good table talk ten or fifteen years later. On the serious side, however, the low points have given me as a parent the depth and dimension I have needed and have taught me and my husband to truly work with the Lord in the awesome task of rearing children. We have seen His hand in our affairs. We know that prayers are answered, that fasting does bring results, that miracles do happen. Time and patience and tender loving care over the years have solved other problems for us. Sometimes just the determination to never give up— to keep on trying—has made the difference. And we are not through yet. Our younger children still have much growing to do, and there will be more ups and downs.

My feelings parallel those of Ralph W. Sockman, who said, "There are parts of a ship which, taken by themselves, would sink. The engine would sink. The propeller would sink. But when the parts of a ship are built together, they float. So it is with the events of my life. Some have been tragic. Some have been happy. But when they are built together they form a craft which is going someplace, and I am comforted."

When things are in order in one's life and home, it can be rewarding to reach out and serve others. After I've met the needs of my family and home, I turn to my neighbors and friends and ward members. Such service is not an escape from duties at home, but rather a further fulfillment of my life. A homemaker must not neglect things at home in order to help others, except in times of true emergencies, if she is to find happiness for herself and blessings for her family.

Today, there seems to be more opposition to happiness than ever before. But there is also more opportunity for happiness. The best (and worst) of everything is available. We'll find the best not by turning in, but by reaching out and growing, trying, learning, improving, stretching, serving, and allowing the Lord to work through us to bless others. He wants it this way, for He says, "Inasmuch as ye have done it unto one of the least of these my brethren, ye have done it unto me." (Matthew 25:40.)

The second requirement for happiness, to *reach up,* is illustrated in this poem by Harry Kemp:

> Chief of all thy wondrous works, O God,
> Supreme of all thy plan,
> Thou hast put an upward reach
> Into the heart of man.

The way to reach up, I believe, is to make the Godhead the center of our lives. With this as our focus, everything else will fall into perspective. No matter what takes place, no matter what trials, tribulations, or tests come our way, we can endure or overcome them through implicit faith in a loving Father in heaven and our Savior, Jesus Christ.

In reaching up, we will choose to read the scriptures as well as other edifying books instead of wasting our time on publications that will pollute our thoughts and drag us down. We will choose to go to the temple, where pure intelligence and peace and joy can be found, or spend our time in other noble pursuits, rather than succumb to the lures of mediocre and immoral television programs or movies that may desensitize us to the point of weakness. All too often the adversary works through such media to present ninety-nine truths in order to put over one gross error. The problems of the world come upon those who have thus made themselves vulnerable.

We will be faithful and valiant in the Church because of conversion, commitment, and consecration to gospel principles, not just because it is a good way of life and a superior social order. We will be converted to Jesus Christ, not just to the Church.

We will know what it is to supplicate the Lord in mighty prayer, rather than to just say our prayers. We will truly fast, not just starve. There is much more to observing the law of the fast, if we are to receive its true benefits, than just going without meals.

We will choose to reach up to overcome our weaknesses and solve our problems rather than allow complacency and rationalization to keep us down. We will understand that repentance and progression are the stepping-stones to exaltation. The way is slow and we may stumble en route, but if we keep headed in the right direction, we'll get there.

We must always strive to keep our thoughts and actions on the highest plane possible. Only at that elevation is true happiness found. The higher we climb, the happier we'll be. As the Prophet Joseph Smith expressed it, "The nearer man approaches perfection, the clearer are his views, the greater his enjoyments."

In conclusion, may I share an impressive example of a truly happy people—in fact, they were the happiest people who have ever lived. These people were so affected by a visit of the resurrected Savior that they found unsurpassed happiness through both reaching out and reaching up. We read:

"And they had all things common among them; therefore there were not rich and poor, bond and free, but they were all made free, and partakers of the heavenly gift. . . .

"And they were married, and given in marriage, and were blessed according to the multitude of the promises which the Lord had made unto them.

"And they did not walk any more after the performances and ordinances of the law of Moses; but they did walk after the commandments which they had received from their Lord and their God, continuing in fasting and prayer, and in meeting together oft both to pray and to hear the word of the Lord. . . .

"And it came to pass that there was no contention in the land, because of the love of God which did dwell in the hearts of the people.

"And there were no envyings, nor strifes, nor tumults, nor whoredoms, nor lyings, nor murders, nor any manner of lasciviousness; and *surely there could not be a happier people among all the people who had been created by the hand of God."* (4 Nephi 1:3, 11-12, 15-16; italics added.)

Happiness does come through reaching out and reaching up. It does matter that we are happy and of good cheer. The Lord assures us, "Men are, that they might have joy." (2 Nephi 2:25.) That is how life is supposed to be!

Appendix

Know How to File It and Find It Again

As homemakers who need to keep track of instructions, warranties, patterns; as community leaders who want to find copies of documents and other items pertaining to their responsibilities; as members of the Church who find special stories or thoughts and want to keep them for future talks or lessons, we all need help. Many persons are great collectors of such materials, but few can ever find what they need quickly. All too often we spend hours, even days, searching through books and papers for specific things. The solution is an effective home filing system.

The system that works best for me is called a *master file system*, patterned after the card catalog at the public library. When you go to the library for a book, you first look up the book's title in the card catalog, where it is listed on various cards according to author, title, and subject. A number then directs you to the proper shelf.

A similar system works beautifully on a smaller scale in a home. I have a small master file, or card catalog, in which every item in my filing cabinet is listed on a four-by-six-inch card. This is done according to title (if there is one), author (if the name is important to me; otherwise I omit that card), and subject (several of them, if necessary). Then a number leads me to the item in my filing cabinet or other storage areas.

In the filing cabinet itself, items are placed in order numerically. I have about twenty-five items in each file folder, so each folder is neither too thick nor too thin. The first manila folder holds items 1 to 25; the second, 26 to 50; and

so forth. In other words, I place items in the filing cabinet
in the order in which I get them. In any one folder contain-
ing twenty-five items, there might be twenty-five nonrelated
subjects. The *master card file* serves as an index to help
me locate a particular item. Even though this system may
appear to be involved at first, it makes sense as soon as it is
thoroughly understood, and it is simple and fast to use. For
supplies you need:

1. A container for your file entries. A pasteboard box
works well, if you don't wish to buy a filing cabinet; you may

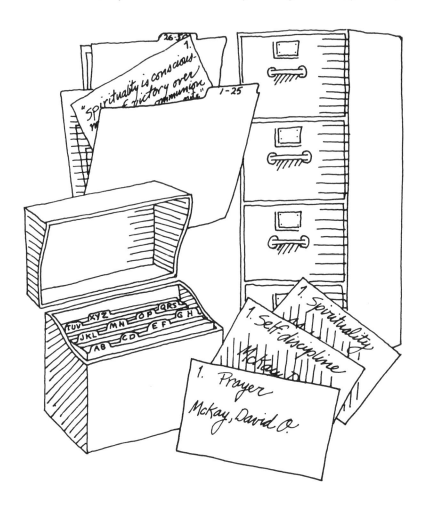

also be able to find an inexpensive secondhand file. I prefer a legal-size filing cabinet, which is two inches larger than the standard size.

2. Manilla folders or more durable plastic folders found in many office supply stores.

3. A small file box for your master file.

4. A supply of four-by-six-inch file cards.

5. Some four-by-six-inch dividers with alphabetized tabs.

With the aid of detailed instructions and illustrations, let's go through the actual steps of filing an item. Let's say I want to place in my file the following quotation by David O. McKay: "Spirituality is consciousness of victory over self and communion with the infinite."

If this is the first entry in my file, I place the arabic numeral 1 in the upper right-hand corner of the entry. Next, I make several index cards for the master file, with the subjects under which I might look for this quotation: Spirituality, Self-Discipline, Prayer, and so forth. I also make a card for the author: McKay, David O. I then place the index cards alphabetically in the master file, and finally I place the quotation itself in the first file folder and put it in my filing cabinet or whatever container I'm using.

Some of the advantages and bonus features of the master file system are:

1. It simplifies decision making. I can list an item according to the title, author, and subject. Many items don't have a clearly defined subject; others are a composite of several topics; and some are just generally edifying. This index system eliminates the frustration of categorizing items and then locating them. The system is workable because I can locate things from various angles. For example, in my file is an excellent article on stewardship that is indexed under Priesthood Order, Marriage, and Obedience, as well as Stewardship. If it were listed under stewardship only, I might forget its significant application to marriage.

2. The system doesn't require much time to set it up and keep it current. All I need to do is pick up one item to be filed,

place a number on it in the upper right-hand corner, make out the index cards, and place it in the file folder. By doing this each time I find something I wish to keep, think of the wealth of material I can file in five or ten years!

3. The system allows for materials of all shapes and sizes. Not only does the master file direct me to items in my filing cabinet, but it also reminds me of special passages in books on my bookshelves (listed by chapter and page on the index cards), games in a cabinet, posters, maps, or any other oversized items that don't fit into the filing cabinet. It is also a handy place to note where I keep a list of storage items, such as clothing for children to grow into, holiday decorations, carpet and wallpaper remnants, and other miscellaneous things that are located in my attic, basement, garage, or elsewhere. In other words, a master file can serve as a reference source for anything in my home.

I have a schoolteacher friend who was frustrated because she had many teaching supplies at school as well as in her home. Her problem was solved when she listed all of her supplies in a master file. The next time Halloween came around, for example, she pulled out the Halloween card and was instantly reminded of all her decorations and materials and where they were located.

4. This system allows for some items to be grouped together. If certain things are always used together, they can be placed in one envelope and given one number. Decorating ideas for the home, roadmaps, warranties, and similar instructions for operating appliances are types of items that can easily be grouped together. I have a folder for Old Testament pictures, one for New Testament, one for principles of the gospel, one for nature, one for family and holiday pictures, and so forth.

In one drawer of my filing cabinet I also have a box with ideas for children's rainy-day fun. There is a small box for birthday party ideas and another for bridal and baby shower favors, games, and invitations. Whenever I get a clever invitation, favor, placecard, or such from a party, I bring it home—gumdrops and all—secure in a plastic bag, and drop it in the labeled container in my file for future inspiration.

5. This master file system provides ideas for talks or lessons. Frequently one of our children will report that he has been asked to give a talk. The most difficult part of a talk is finding a subject to talk about, so we just thumb through the master file, and within a few minutes he has selected a subject and is enthusiastically developing it. When I flip through my master file for lessons or talks, I can usually find just the right stories, poems, scriptural references, and thoughts.

6. Anyone in the family can make use of the file. I keep a small card in front of the file upon which family members jot down what they have taken from the file to make certain that it is returned. It's easy to borrow something from the file, use it, and then tuck it into a book and forget to return it to the file; the "checkout" card helps prevent this.

The master file system as explained here can be developed and refined for any home. Ours is all ready to be programmed into a home computer! One word of caution, however: be highly selective in what you file. Don't file something just because it is in print. Make certain that it is worth keeping and using again. The wastebasket should play an important role in your project.

Here are some questions I've been asked about this system, with my answers:

Question: Do you place more than one entry on each index card?

Answer: I do, while some people do not. Obviously, some cards are fuller than others. By listing more than one entry on a card, I find it is much faster to see what is available and how much material is on file on a particular subject. This also greatly reduces the number of cards needed in the master file.

Question: How do you handle bulky items for filing?

Answer: Usually bulky items, such as books, are kept on a shelf with a reference to them in the master file. Some small booklets are placed directly in my filing cabinet, however.

Question: What about very small items?

Answer: If something is so small that it might become lost in the manila folder, I either recopy it on a large piece of paper or card or paste it on a larger sheet of paper or card.

Question: Do you number over again with each drawer in your filing cabinet?

Answer: Yes, I do. Otherwise the digits get too high. I handle this by numbering each drawer with a roman numeral—I, II, III, IV. Then the file items go from 1 to 750 in each drawer.

Question: Are you ever unable to locate something because you can't remember the author or title and are vague about the specific subjects?

Answer: Rarely. When this happens, I quickly flip through the master file until I find it.

Question: Do you file only gospel-oriented items?

Answer: Yes, but to me the gospel is all-inclusive. Remember, we seek after anything that is "virtuous, lovely, or of good report or praiseworthy." I do have a separate file for my recipes, however, and a separate file for financial records.

Question: Should children be encouraged to start files?

Answer: Yes, definitely! I started my file as a teenager, and a young girl in our neighborhood was excited one Christmas to receive filing supplies from her parents as a gift.

Index